The poems in *Quince, Rose,* [...] ruminations on the lifelong sea[...] [...] p[...] [...] meaning. They are often contemplative, as in "Wakeful on Thirty-third Street," where a pair of strangers cross paths while walking in the rain before dawn. Water is omnipresent in its many forms—even juxtaposing the danger and potency of the Pacific Ocean with the still tedium of dishwater, in "Submerged," where a lifelong fear ends in at least the possibility of redemption. Toward the end of the collection, the sense of loss that serves as a low undercurrent throughout is crystallized in "Federal Building Bombed," where a rescue worker is ultimately brought to tears by a cup of coffee, faced with "the only grief/ I could put my/ hands around." Ultimately, though, the prevailing feeling is one of hope.

—LEAH BROWNING
editor of the *Apple Valley Review*

Quince, Rose, Grace of God is a fabulous collection of poetry. It is an audacious and evocative work drawing upon a strong sense of life and humanity. *Quince, Rose, Grace of God* is clever as well. Trina Gaynon skillfully employs the use of metaphor to create vivid imagery of horticulture, ecology, and humanity. One cannot help but imagine having not only a visceral experience with her poems but a deeply emotional one as well. "Invocation Dusk" brilliantly, with its powerful sense of compassion, establishes the emotional context for *Quince, Rose, Grace of God* as it invites the reader to consider what is to follow on subsequent pages. Poem after poem, Trina Gaynon weaves various narratives between the imaginative and the empirical, between the concrete and the abstract, between what readers know to be the human experience. This poet would be remiss by not saying bravo to Trina Gaynon and *Quince, Rose, Grace of God*.

—EMMETT WHEATFALL
poet, *Our Scarlet Blue Wounds*

Trina Gaynon's collection, *Quince, Rose, Grace of God*, explores the human puzzle of learning to live in this world and what to do with its often-contradictory lessons. Her invocation, "Remember to stake the peonies/ bury iris bulbs in October/ hold the world in your poetry/ make it sacred," advises that life is both practical and spiritual. It is a world of beauty—pink flowers and western sunsets— but also one in which fishermen husbands may not return, and even opening one's door in the morning could reveal things we don't want to see. The book is not rooted in one place but reflects the author's travels and relocations—New England, Tennessee, the ruins of the Oklahoma Federal Building bombing, San Francisco, South Carolina, a lobster-fishing coast, O'Keeffe's New Mexico— an American kind of wandering. Yet even for a lost fisherman, we can imagine, "There are enough hard-boiled detective books below to tide him over." In any case, we are on our own, and we make what we can of it all. "Heading west, where God lives, I glow, sheltering the flame of the holy, burning most brightly alone on the road."

—Barbara Drake
author of *What We Say to Strangers* and *The Road to Lilac Hill*

Quince, Rose, Grace of God

Trina Gaynon

Fernwood
PRESS

Quince, Rose, Grace of God

©2024 by Trina Gaynon

Fernwood Press
Newberg, Oregon
www.fernwoodpress.com

Printed in the United States of America

Cover and page design: Mareesa Fawver Moss
Cover image provided by The Miriam and Ira D. Wallach Division of Art, Prints and
Photographs: Print Collection, The New York Public Library
Author photo: Irene Perezchica

ISBN 978-1-59498-134-0

Dedicated to:
My mother, who showed me the joy of being creative,
and my father, who imprinted me with the love of books and learning

Table of Contents

Invocation 11

Mockingbird Notes 13
   Spring Incantation 14
   Migration Routes..15
   Snow Melts, Tennessee...17
   No Clemency..19
   Peaceable Kingdom.. 20
   Sweet Contamination 21
   Eventide, Naomi..23
   Through Her Husband's Eyes 24
   The Threat of Drowning..25

Faded Pink Ladies 27
   Wife of a Prison Gardener..28
   Submerged 30
   Sand and Ash 32
   Monarchs 33
   Distracted...34
   Winter Departure..36
   Last Prayer 37
   Offering Respite..38

Large Hungers, Lean Purses 39
   Spring in the City 40
   Rear Window..41
   Infectious Paranoia...42
   Pacific Bell Comes Calling 43
   Open Reading,
   Shattuck Avenue Bakery 44
   Angel Island, San Francisco 45
   Tor House 47
   Una Jeffers' Tower 48
   The Road Alone 49
   Celibacy... 50

Long Train Whistle...51
   Badlands 52
   After the Fireworks 53
   Once Begun...54
   Language Lessons..55
   Down the Road..56
   Difficult to Place...58
   October..59
   Lecture Devant la Fenetre Ouverte 60
   Prayers for the Barren 61
   Eclipse...64
   Hunger Moon 65
   Wakeful on Thirty-third Street 66
   What Does the New Moon Hide From? 67
   In the Light..68
   One More Draft..69

Slow Burn 71

    Downsizing 72

    Down the Mountain 73

    Beauty Ranch 76

    Alluvial Changes 78

    Holy Places 79

    Austere Essentials of the Palette 81

    Some Stars Are Not Used for Navigation 83

    The Catch 85

    Shattered 86

    Federal Building Bombed 87

    Nicodemus 88

Acknowledgments 89

Title Index 91

First Line Index 95

Invocation

White peonies blooming along the porch
send out light
while the rest of the yard grows dim.

　　　　—"Peonies at Dusk," Jane Kenyon

Soft family whispers
　　　　nightstand lamp shines
　　　　　　　　early spring

Missing—
　　　　porch, early poppies, rain
Without me—
　　　　hummingbirds and burgundy hollyhocks,
　　　　the burdened pear tree
Leaving—
　　　　books, Donald,
　　　　the battle to keep the wood stove alight,
　　　　New England ghosts,
　　　　the cancer, the cancer

Remember to stake the peonies
　　　　bury iris bulbs in October
　　　　　　　　hold the world in your poems
　　　　　　　　　　　　make it sacred

Mockingbird Notes

Spring Incantation

Learn the names of all you love—quince, rose, grace
of God. Chant them as you walk city streets—
aspen, iris, Monterey pine. Call them
by name, hush their voices—crowing rooster,
German shepherd, Stephanie, Kimberly—
who live at the top of their lungs. Beneath
the sound of the wind in old aspen branches,
repeat the names you know—blackberry, sun-
shine, chickadee. Pray these wage battle
against angry voices—seagull, orange blossom,
morning glory. Seek the names of those you
do not know that you may come to love them—
spider flower, leopard's bane, boys who give
each other bloody noses in the playground.

Migration Routes

Down south, Mama keeps a trio
of hummingbird feeders,
the syrup she uses sweeter,
she'll swear, than the neighbor's.
She keeps her cats cloistered
indoors, away from fights and prey.

Across country, Daddy makes the rounds,
filling his feeders to gather
finches, cardinals, and squirrels
in the yard. He greases
wires the squirrels use
to reach the seed. It works once.
The squirrel slips off. The next
one hangs on, running upside down,
spring hungry.

Even the clock in his kitchen thinks
it's an aviary, a different bird song
for every hour, the same song at the same
time every day.

I sleep through mockingbird
notes rising toward the moon.
But I waken earlier now
that the birds have returned,
my eyes on the alarm clock
even before their songs start,
its digital numbers red in gray light.

Perhaps the cat's anticipation wakes me;
she stretches, sharpens her claws
on the armchair by the bed, and jumps
up on me, as the birdsong begins.

Long before the cat arrived,
I grew discouraged with filling
bird feeders every morning. These days,
I refuse to lure birds for her. Still
they come for blackberries.

Snow Melts, Tennessee

The dalmatian eats with horses,
their trough filled with warm feed.

But the orange tomcat lopes across
the yard to walk with my sister and me,

until he scents prey in the woods that
edge the bottom. A volley of gunshots

in the distance marks the progress
of other hunters. And birds scatter.

Last time we walked through snowfall
together, we were teenagers here.

Pigs huddle near the barn, their grunts
crossing the field more softly

than our boots in mud-soft grass.
Twyla hears them long before I do,

their grunts as hushed as our breath,
mere smoke in the air. Crystal daggers

edge the oak leaf in her hand.
In the cemetery, charred ground marks

where oak leaves were raked together
and burned. Our feet can no longer

scuffle through them and disturb
the dead in winter. Shadows of marble

headstones protect the frost,
ice cathedrals hidden in dry grass.

The sound of wind across the top
of a stand of pines provides the psalms.

I am more at home among the dead
than my sister, who walks delicately,

as though her feet feel their bones.
If I wake them, the dead might speak

about what outlasts winter here,
before we leave our family behind us.

No Clemency

Asked about the day of my birth,
my mother tells me the plot
of last night's John Wayne movie,
the one where a father shoots his son
to save him from a life of crime.

On that Tuesday in 1957:
my mother's water broke in front
of guests. I waited to arrive
until seven that night, a short labor,
a polite after-dinner appearance.

California's governor refused
to stay the execution
of the kidnapper and murderer
of a fourteen-year-old girl.

Playboy swindler's sentence changed.
Not thirty days in county jail
with five years of probation
but one to ten in San Quentin.

Three men died of suffocation
when Little Rock excavation caved in.
Thirty died in Burma in a train wreck
after rail tracks sabotaged.

And it always rains on March the fifth.

Peaceable Kingdom

For Evelyn, my stepmother

David's never seen a goat pen before.
Well-camouflaged in jeans and his father's pullover,
he freezes for the camera, his smile genuine.
The goats pay him no-never-mind.
Also featured on this farm tour—the hen house
producing several hundred eggs a week,
shared with long-haired rabbits as permanent guests.
A sow and her piglets rest next door.
Up the hill, a mare and colt lip hay
stacked next to the trailer Cheyenne calls home.
General, a Great Dane standing up to our guide's chest,
joins us in our march as Cheyenne whips up and down
the gravel drive, making sure we miss none of the highlights.

Sweet Contamination

Before she clasps
the silver support of the bus,
she takes a tissue
in her gloved hand
to keep the white cotton clean.

She leans over
to whisper secrets in the cave
of the ear of her daughter,
a teenager with her face
shadowed
by unruly hair.

Once, I wanted to go through
the world this way, never
touching it,
whispering.
But I came to love
cool steel poles and the echoes
my voice makes when it strikes
the window
on the other side.

The mother
frowns
at men who
cast
their eyes on her daughter,
shelters the seated girl with her body.

I surrendered such shelter,
meant to keep me beyond the reach
of men's hunger,

for I came to love their groaned
responses to a glimpse of flesh.
I came to love
the inescapable scent
every mother must know
her daughter hides.

Eventide, Naomi

Tonight, with my eyes tired
from reading the boys' lessons
and my hands sore
from weeding blackberries,
the colors in my quilt
dance, delirious with the love of God.
My fingers push the needle
along a diamond in a square,
find rest in a pattern
as old as the Amish.
Aaron and I measure our days
with plowing and seeding,
milking and churning.
The days are not as long
as they need to be,
the hours not as long as
the clock would make them.
Tonight, a blister forms
on a callused forefinger,
as I listen to Aaron's
voice rise and fall
with the scriptures,
and I work a little longer
on the quilt that will go
with my daughter
to the home of her marriage.

Through Her Husband's Eyes

Remember her
sitting under
the glowing pepper tree
on this May afternoon
all your life.
Peruvian flute music
circles the square
where you come
to rest
in the shade.

Listen with your eyes closed.
The cathedral's blue dome
touches the sky.

The Threat of Drowning

The sea spits him back out at the end
of each long day spent lobstering,
just long enough to sell the day's catch
and fill the house with the smell
of the sea again. Though he showers
and puts on dry jeans and flannel to come
home, when the wood stove warms him,
sea salt leaches out of pores
in his wind-reddened face.

The sea blurs his vision long after
he closes the door and sits down
to supper—a lobster bisque.
It's all he can do to swallow
the soup before his eyes close
and his soft snores cross
the room, the way the sea
crosses the sand and reaches
for our house at high tide.

Who eases into bed beside me
hours later, the lobsterman or the sea?

Faded Pink Ladies

Wife of a Prison Gardener

She doesn't walk down to the beach
anymore, though we can hear the surf
in her living room, the windows closed.
She doesn't climb the townhouse stairs
either, to the loft where children sleep.
The sound of the quarrels rises

when her husband gets home. Smoke rises
from cigarettes like fog from the beach
until beer and anger put them to sleep,
while sea lions bark on rocks in the surf
and the dog pads up and down stairs
until it is sure all human eyes are closed.

Her husband sleeps on the sofa, the closed
bedroom door between them, until he rises
to leave for work. She calls up the stairs,
promises the children a trip to the beach
to get them up. So they wait for a low surf
to make it safe enough for her to go to sleep

over a detective novel or just go to sleep,
the six-pack empty, the small cooler closed.
She's always aware of her fear of the surf,
afraid of what happens when the tide rises.
So when it's time to take them to the beach,
she doesn't wake them from their nap upstairs.

Sometimes when she's alone inside, she stares
through windows reflecting loss, then sleeps
again because she hates to see herself beached
in a Northern California town on 101; closed
in by redwoods and the ocean, her anger rises
only briefly, then drowns, a rock in the surf.

Mostly, she is numbed by the rhythm of the surf
and the television at which the children stare
for hours, as if early cartoons were sunrises
full of wonder, like dreams while they sleep.
She prays to see the turreted prison closed
down, she and her family removed from the beach.

She watches surfers on floating boards, half asleep,
tries not to stare at nakedness brought so close.
The fearful sea rises; she turns away from the beach.

Submerged

The third time, to reach her it hid
in waves and rip currents,
then went for her husband, washed him off
a rock while he fished at Morro Bay,
in front of the sons he left standing
on the hard stone beach,
while she watched from the kitchen window,
up to her elbows in dishwater.
She called the coast guard;
she held the boys in her arms.
Relieved that it was finished with her,
she thought that after such a loss
there was nothing left to fear,
until she identified the body,
in a room with no one but the coroner
to hold her up when the dark closed in.

The first time, it nearly took her at twelve,
when she ran off into the deep
end of the pool, chasing a beach ball,
and after the shock of the splash,
the water closed softly around her body
and over her head. She was blue
with the weight of still water
and lack of air, beating her arms
against the lid closing in over her,
until her cousin pulled her out.

It tried again when her husband coaxed
her to lower her body into a man-made lake;
exchanging air bubbles for water-filled lungs,
she fought to grab the side of the boat

and pull her weight out of the green murk
on realizing that only hundred-year-old
trees could rise through the mud and fish
to branch in sunlight
and still touch the silty bottom.

After that, she never opened
her eyes underwater, afraid
to see it waiting,
believing it lurked there just for her.
She kept her head up, never took
the children beyond where she could plant
her feet on cool tile at the bottom of the pool.

Once she had buried her husband, she excised
fishing poles from the house, kept
her younger son off surfboards, and refused
to watch sunsets at Carmel when the older boy
bought a beach house, becoming its ally.
She refused to travel coast roads.
She shrank further and further into the city,
tunneling from work to home by subway.

So when God called, she wouldn't answer.
It left her alone for years, and she believed
either God had a hand in the drowning
or there was no God. She'd been in church
every Sunday beside her husband
and lived without God all that time.
Why did he call her name now,
talking baptism, telling her
it was time to immerse herself,
to open her eyes underwater and live?

Sand and Ash

Awake with a new design, I walk
to the studio in the cold—to draw,
then finger samples of glass.
Winter winds throw themselves
against your window, wooden crosses
nailed at corners to strengthen the frame;

its rotting wood and brittle glass
color my dreams, draw me away
from my wife's restless turning.
Now my wife cannot breathe without
a rush of oxygen forced
into her lungs with a pump.

When the sun rises, your handmade panes
bend light in waves. A medallion in each pane
casts pattern on stucco walls.
You painted clear glass indigo to block
the view: a redwood gym set, a rental house,
laundry always drying on the clothesline.

I can't see God through glass
either, as once I did when I pieced
his promises together with lead.
Grief is no dark thing, but blinding
light that leaves no shadow for shelter,
makes stained glass irrelevant.

My wife grows brittle, muscles atrophy.
When only silence sleeps next to me,
the total eclipse will begin.

Monarchs

Chasing the last of summer
out to the ocean,
past faded pink ladies,

    scrub oak,
    leaning eucalyptus,
    around hills of brown grass,

        and slopes stripped by the wind
        to bare serpentine and granite,
        while above me hawks spiral

           the October updrafts—
           alone, I drive past
           horses in salt meadows

               and miss the boy who refused
               to chase summer with me,
               who was afraid to rise

early enough to find the blast
of the sun balanced
by the moon's quarter.

               Monarch butterflies flutter
               in the air, always moving
               away from the ocean.

                  I walk the beach,
                  the sand warm on my feet,
                  the surf winter cold.

The sun reflected in tide pools
is as bright as the one
in the sky and as ungraspable.

33

Distracted

You pull ripe tomatoes
from the vines and a few
of the plentiful zucchini,
plan how many you need to fill
the waiting quart jars with sauce,
then contemplate the lean body
of a bicyclist bent
low over handlebars
as he races past your garden.
You bend over to unearth garlic
and ponder making love to a man
who rides a mountain bike home
in the unspeakably blue twilight,
his white hands gleaming.
Inside, at the butcher's block,
you peel, seed, chop
each tomato, its skin tight
from the stroke of the sun
and long drinks of water,
then linger over a memory
of the June morning
that sunlight revealed
another bicyclist, thighs
tightened by the effort
of riding uphill, arms tan,
a few gray hairs among the brown.
He brought you Irish poetry,
a taste for shandy, and the lyrical
pronunciation of the word *shyte*.
Brown the onions in oil heated slowly.
Add garlic, tomatoes, bay, and thyme.

Simmer gently. Spoon
into quart jars, seal them
in the pressure cooker,
and listen to the hiss
of steam escaping, reminding
you of how often you missed
something he said
in a voice so soft you never
learned to listen hard enough.

Winter Departure

The early light reflects the short gray hairs
among the brown, and still he's just a boy
of twenty-five, who rises slowly, turns
to stare down at the bed where she coils
asleep, the dreamless sleep that only comes
on nights when he has filled her up with rain.
He brought it with him out of Dublin slums
to blanket California hills in gray
soft shrouds. He waits for gold to turn to green.
He lingers over tea and toast until
he's read the *Times*. Packing his bag to leave,
he has no ties to things that keep her still
beneath their weight—a job, this house, her car.
It's almost Christmas, and Ireland's not so far.

Last Prayer

God, I can gather Lincoln roses in my arms and
leave
this garden.

My left heel forces
my shovel into clay.

God, hear me. I can
leave
this body I live in.

Tired of working alone,
heart full of splinters,

I pray.
Where are you?

You fill the house with the scent of daylily,
give me a new crop of blackberry vines
to root out,

then abandon me to my longing
for a man to share the perfume and the digging
out of strong old roots.

A shadow on the lawn,
cast by cajuput trees,

you wander
away from my heart, land, and house.

Damn it.
What do I get if I stay?
The raw, dark anger
in my tomatoes and unbreakable sod?

Offering Respite

The first morning spring winds
rise, the camellia calls me
to clear away dead leaves
and blackberry vines encouraged
by winter rains. Spiders lumber
through unmown grass
wearing their hourglasses
and long legs; yet Christ,
coming through the redwood gate,
is tired. Lent begins,
a preparation for death,
with no assurance of resurrection.
He fears that he should have
touched more lepers, driven out
more demons, spent more time
on his knees in gardens like this.

I offer him the things
that heal me—chimes
scaling the wind, mint crushed
underfoot. Come watch
the peach tree bloom.
It doesn't need you.
Sit cross-legged on a sun-warmed
stone wall. Its reflected
silence presses on your skin.
Rest in my arms. Sleep away
your doubts about tomorrow.
And when the rain comes
alongside the lingering dawn,
rescue nothing more than
roses threatened by mildew;
bring them to the breakfast table.

Large Hungers, Lean Purses

Spring in the City

Once again, rain falls late into the night.
Plum-tree blossoms wait to be battered.
Away from branches, the petals cling to shingles,
making winter-worn roofs ornate beneath wood smoke

from chimneys. With no stars to brighten the spring sky,
cold and wordless poets meditate about warmer days.
When the storm ends and the fruit sets this year,
skunks will mark the air to court and mate in the dark.

Young men in dingy city bars drink away the short nights.
Their eager energy spills through the stuffy rooms.
I abandon restless boys while they search
for a narrow woman to sate until sleep overtakes them.

Behind me, a face glimpsed in the corner of the bar
separates from the crowd and the neon lights. I decide
not to follow the hypnotic eyes, while pollen moves up
the hills on skyscraper winds, finds no one to irritate.

Daffodil blooms fall beneath the rain's weight.
It's me the scent will captivate, even overwhelm.
At the mercy of the ancient messages of lilacs,
it's me the scent will elevate into the night.

Rear Window

That full moon catches
a neighbor seeking
guitar chords and singing,
softening a voice that
comes over and down
other windows flushed
with light but no discernible
motion, the air heavier with
the roar of jets on takeoff
than her music. The musician
stops, calls out for a kitten,
then lowers the window.

A spider is only a moving
shadow along the post, a tickle
up the spine. The gunman was
taken away last night,
disappeared with the SWAT
team and bullhorns. Now it's
just me and the spider, changing
shadows as the set goes dark.

Infectious Paranoia

This year, when the lily of the Nile blooms,
my neighbor no longer crawls out her door
after dark to chomp off the buds.
Even anxiety evolves to higher planes,
and now she screams death threats
over the phone to the FBI,
where only a machine listens,
and she believes an electrical short
in her ancient Honda
may be a car bomb
and abandons it in the driveway.
There is no insulation
to separate me from the screaming
at two and six in the morning.
Yet yesterday, she leaned in her doorway
and asked about our rent raise,
as she remarked on the beauty
of my gladiolas, shades of pink.
I begin to keep an eye out for missing buds.

Pacific Bell Comes Calling

He drives up in a Pac Bell truck,
ready to repair my phone service,
though 611 said my instrument
was at fault, my twenty-dollar phone.
He bellies up to the outside wall,
hugging the paint to avoid
the spines of an ancient cactus
and the kitchen window, swung open
to air out the Saturday morning smell
of fried potato and onions.
Finding no problem in the gray box
that splits the wires coming into the house,
he climbs a ladder he leans
against the brick wall that separates us
from looming apartment buildings
and swings up the spiked pole
into ponderosa pine branches,
where a limb weighs down the black wire
bringing electric pulses to me.
He reaches out to clip the taut wires,
lets them fall toward the house.
I lose my ability then to call out,
as I had lost the ability to receive
calls only days before.
While he replaces the wires, I take
a walk, looking back to see him
smiling, standing in a shaft of sunshine
and rolling up a piece of cable.

Open Reading,
Shattuck Avenue Bakery

The new manager is atwitter
with reminders
to exercise caution
going down the back stairs
to the bathroom in the corner
of the working bakery
that turns out
10,000 croissants a day
and gallons of coffee
for free refills.
The chest beneath
the Yale sweatshirt
decompresses
when he is assured
that the customers don't bite
or slide down banisters.
This blessing and this curse:
may your house be filled
with poets
with their large hungers
and lean purses.

Angel Island, San Francisco

The island watches the moss grow
over the stone steps and foundations,
plants eucalyptus striplings
where once wooden floors rotted,
keeps that silver guardian ghost
reaching for the cloudless sky
with a multitude of bare branches
and a sprinkling of velvet-green nuts.

The island knows drought deep inside itself,
holds water back from fountains,
recognizes the cleansing salt water
that surrounds it as invasive.
Native oaks and foreign eucalyptus,
a row of palms bordering the bay,
and conifers, dropping slippery blankets
of needles over dry grass, thrive.

The island uses the voices of captives
inscribed on wooden barracks' walls
to say words the dusty white and pink
flowerings of eucalyptus cannot.
In China Cove, the island has heard
Miwok, Spanish, Chinese, German,
and English spoken; it answered
back with rustling winds.

The island reacts in surprise
to one set of steep stairs ending not
at a door but a fence topped in barbed wire,
to direct the tourists to another door
and to state that migration
may prove to be a fruitless trek,
failure met just outside the door,
and the long trip home sorrowful.

Tor House

My ghost you needn't look for; it is probably
Here, but a dark one, deep in the granite, not dancing on wind
With the mad wings and the day moon.

—Robinson Jeffers

A moment ago, Lee sat at the table
just inside the sun-flooded French doors,
lingered over a cup of coffee, and breathed
deeply the smoke from the wood fire.
She watched the guests walk carefully along
the brick paths of her late father-in-law's garden.

They come hourly on weekends
to try to understand a poet
who built a tower just because.
An ill-assorted lot, this noon group,
two couples staring at artifacts
brought back from New Mexico or Peking
and scattered among primroses.

One woman spouts forth her knowledge of stone;
she separates it from poetry, turns it into hard fact.
Her tall and silent companion knows the poetry
as a scholar, knows the facts of the poet's life like stone.

Earlier, Lee watched the other couple from her bedroom;
seated together in a car, windows down, an hour early.
They huddled over a book, read to each other.
The young woman walked away, the joy of the sun in her eyes.
He read on, undisturbed by the birds, unaware of Lee.
They are the kind who will sneak away from the docent
to sit in the poet's chair a moment and hear stone breathe.

Una Jeffers' Tower

Robert climbs the secret stairs of the tower last,
his eyes the only light, as left shoulder first,
he follows the curve of the stones all around him.
A little fearful the passage will be too narrow,
I look down and see his belly just skim the rocks.

Jeffers collected native stone on this land
to build his Rapunzel, his stolen wife, a tower,
a place for her to sit and look down across the lawn
at her ex-husband's house and his newer wives,
to watch the sea reflect sky and listen
to her twin sons play in the cool stone room below,
the room whose only purpose was to buttress
the rest of the tower against its own weight
and winds that do not confine their power to surf.

Robert wants to shout at the seagulls and our guide,
to ask a dozen questions about the poet and the pulley
that lifted rocks into place from a wheelbarrow
to salute Irish Tors, private places, and love.
Robert is bewildered by quiet reverence.

The Road Alone

Traveling the Camino Real,
Robert still crossed himself
before altars of missions,
though he'd been unconfessed for years—

happiest in a car, concentrating
on the swoop of tree-lined avenues,
autumn flashing by on oak and cherry
and sweet gums, red, green, yellow, red.

He taught me to choose the road
that led out of town, then crossed
into new territory. So I head
for the curve of the San Rafael Bridge

and Mount Tam with the pink clouds beyond.
Neither God nor Robert ever promised me
that I'd never leave town alone again.
Though I left Robert years ago,

sometimes there's a vacuum in my life,
and I try to fill it with the whish
of the car past windbreaks of trees.
I'm angry at both of us until

the wind along the car shears
away anger. With nothing but the bay
below me and the golden hills before me—
like a kerosene lamp lit by a match, I glow.

Heading west, where God lives,
I glow, sheltering the flame of the holy,
burning most brightly alone on the road,
silent, sometimes walking, sometimes flying.

Celibacy

She thought they were making love,
but what she heard the strangers doing
was leaning against the closed door of a bedroom
in the midst of an orgasm that made the timber frame
of the house shiver. In her dream,
she entered this house unsure of what made it quake
so gently. It'd been a while since she'd been in a bed
or a home so moved by passion. It was a sorrowful thing
to be in such a place but not part of the heat,
embarrassing to the hearer of something so private
gone public, and the listener so hungry for it.

I am so tired of hearing the lovers,
groaning for deeper, wider pleasure,
tired of being safe and warm and calm.
What I want is to be inside the groan.

Long Train Whistle

Badlands

Eating oranges, she crossed Death Valley,
left her car and began walking along the road,
a pilgrim on the edge of the salt waste
with its ravens. The grit of dunes blew around her.

Staring into shadowed arroyos, she stood
on the rim of the Grand Canyon, snow captured
in her hair—the rest of her swaddled against the cold.
The wind bent mesquite and carved granite.

Here in Richmond where the canyon winds left her,
she closes the door of her stucco house behind her.
She walks out on a half-finished poem, photograph
albums of those trips. She's looking for another edge.

She walks city streets under a full moon before dawn,
passing leaf-stripped trees and bakery vans. Boot heels
tap out restless prayers against concrete. Prayers rise
to vanishing stars. The horizon becomes a pink halo.

After the Fireworks

After camping alone for a week,
I load up the van and head home
through the Santa Cruz Mountains.
I want to tell you again that I love
the dry gold before me, as I did last year
as we headed across the Martinez Bridge
to watch fireworks in Winters,
where the center of town is a square
with a gazebo in need of paint
and a dusty pickup truck parks
behind every farmhouse.

There the Buckhorn served
sourdough bread, butter pats melted
beneath it, and ribs, the barbecue sauce
dripping down our bare arms.
We drove through crowds lined up
to buy fireworks from wooden huts
on every corner. At an empty dirt lot
by the high school, we spread ourselves
on the car hood while the world exploded
into dripping sparks one color at a time
and we inhaled gunpowder.

You drift through every few months,
just when I've gotten use to my own
cold feet in bed. Next time you stop by,
I'll have forgotten how I love dry, gold hills,
and winter rain will have begun to turn
the world green again—when
nothing catches fire as easily.

Once Begun

It (painting) got too intense, I turned to horticulture.

—"My Grandmother who Painted," Honor Moore

It stains my forefinger and fills my nails,
slices my palm with burred weeds,
and blisters my love line with tools
required to bring it to submission.
For the dried skin and sore back,
I get stock so heavy that watering
forces aromatic heads downward.
I get nasturtiums creeping
across the stump of ponderosa pine.
I get snapdragons throwing themselves
up along the wall of peeling paint.
Morning glories long to climb
the trellis that's not yet hung.
Tomato vines reach out
to the sun from shade beneath the stairs.
Marigolds battle snails
who munch on young spinach.
Pansies turn their faces to the sky
so that they may grow up to be bushes.
And I get more wild, thick-stalked anise propagating,
propagating faster than I can pull it from the earth.

Language Lessons

The upper room of the church holds
a class of adults learning
English as a second language,
after long hours of work and no dinner.
Below them, their children
play basketball and eat
a snack of ramen noodles
prepared by the oldest girls.
When cleanup is done,
the children are parceled
out to volunteer tutors.

A tutor leans into the text
that includes the former Soviet Union
in its discussion of capitalism
and developed countries.
Just listening to the ninth-grade
girl halt at words split
by syllables at the end of the line
hurts. The tutor cannot wait,
pronounces the words for her,
and is surprised by the music
of his own language. He longs
to tell her that all languages
sing, the one she speaks at home
and the one they are both struggling
with across a table temporarily raised
in the church gym beneath
the basketball hoops.

Down the Road

The tiny mother leaves a daycare job
it took her years to train for.
In Berkeley, she got minimum wage.
What will South Carolina offer,
the Deep South, where most waitresses
make less than minimum wage
and tips are next to nonexistent?

Not long ago, her husband put his fist
through a wall, then left the family
to cut up chickens in a Fresno factory.
He rises at dawn six days a week.
Their daughter Stephanie begged to use
my phone to call him, sure his leaving
was all her fault.

As I gather the last summer roses,
the Laotian grandparents, mother,
and five children ride away in a red van,
on their way to work in furniture factories
in South Carolina. Grandfather will no longer
walk the dog across the street, gathering cans
and water bottles for recycling as he goes.

In South Carolina, they will rejoin their clan,
scattered during immigration. Grandfather
will regain his status among the people.
Beside factory housing, Grandmother
will again plant a vegetable garden
able to defeat all weeds. Green hills
will remind them of the old country.

Kimberly will no longer ring my bell
to ask if we can bake cookies today.
Steven will race his bike on dirt roads.
Stacy, finishing sixth grade, will soon be married.
Michael will be lost in the silence he carries
with him already, and Stephanie will learn
to tell the world to fuck off.

Difficult to Place

He lights a cigarette
when he steps into sunshine
that slants low in his eyes,
and heat from the cigarette
cools the air around him,
creates its own breeze
and its own dry cloud.
You can take the boy off the streets.
But the surf of freeway noise
and whir of jets needle
him into leaving the ranch house
out in the suburbs where County
parked him for another year.

At seventeen, no one
can keep him from spending
nights under the street lamp
in the park where boys
bring their pit bulls
to fight until they're bloody.
No one tries to keep his hands
from under the skirt
of a girl who chooses
to climb into his dented Nova.
He claims you can't take
the boy off the street once
he hears the voices
of summer fire hydrants
thrown wide open.

October

He comes in, hidden in the
                              petals
                    of a Lincoln rose,
                    a rare bumble bee,
          large as my thumb and calm,
              until I drop my rice bowl
              over him. He buzzes as
              loudly as the hovering
                  hummingbird until
                      freed among
                      dragonflies.

Lecture Devant la Fenetre Ouverte

—Oil by Therese Albert

I.

The sun shines away the window frame;
the bottom of a birch tree disappears
into the same white glare
that becomes an autumn meadow.
The book before me disappears
into the brightness that fogs my eyes,
the way the roses in the tablecloth
disappear into the roses on my dress
and the potted cyclamen
fade against the silvered corner post.
My windows need no shades.

II.

Beyond the open window, the French
landscape smudges itself,
the same hay yellow of late-summer
California. Rarely does a portrait
present a woman's shoulders sloping
into a housecoat, her back in shadow,
her face turned away to a book
reflecting the glare of tablecloth
and meadow. All fades before
her hidden eyes but the words, moving
from the page to the cool, dark mind.

Prayers for the Barren

Matins (Waking)

November,
and even after the first winter storm,
rain continues to fill my belly
where there is no child

and no chance of a child.

Hard to believe, with the winter morning
so full of birdsong,
that time kept slipping from my body

one unfertilized egg,
one tissue nest at a time.

Prime

Pink sunrises hurt.
My heart yearns for the East
and for all things beginning.

Tierce (Undern Song)

Surely Sarah at Abraham's side,
filled with grief,

knew my anger
when she laughed at God's promise.

Does God require absolute despair
before the seed can be planted?

Sect (Noon)

I am not alone in this;

single women cluster,
deep in disappointment, deep
in the storehouses of universities
with our coffers of silence.
We have waited for a man who loves us,
who longs for our children, who
would fill our bellies with honor.

Nons (Afternoon)

November,
and I prefer to fill
the neighborhood's children
with chocolate chip cookies
rather than listen to the refrigerator
become the only other breathing
presence in this house

(and sometimes even it is still).

I claim not to miss my lost children
but send the neighbors' little ones,

who see and speak my empty hours,
back into the cold to play.

Vespers (Evening)

I poke up the fire I use to warm the night.
Again this year the apple tree flowered
but dropped its petals in spring rains,

before the bees began their pollinating dance.

Is it time to turn the apple tree
into kindling for next year's fires?

Compline (Past Dark)

My clitoris rises at a glimpse—
neighbors embracing in
front of their window,

thighs and hips entwined in the heat of creation.

Somewhere there is a son to be raised
with joy and despair but no father,

his father only a long train whistle
at another crossing almost beyond my hearing.

Eclipse

No rarity, lunar eclipses,
but often clouds cloak
them or the earth's spin
conceals them, yet this moon
shines clear and full over
East Bay hills and waits
for the earth's slow shadow to fall
across the pock-marked face
and set it glowing red.
The next total lunar eclipse
to be observed from here will occur
in the new millennium
on my fourth-fourth birthday.

Monday, my first mammogram
came back clouded, a shadow
gathered in breast tissue
that I wait for a radiologist
to compress and magnify, then name.
For the first time, it occurs
to me that I might not meet
the new millennium.

As I turn to the sky,
even the fog rolling
over and down from west
of coastal slopes
cannot obscure that moon.

Hunger Moon

This morning, that full hunger
moon still low on the horizon,
a corpse curled up in the park
across the street from my house.

She rested on a bench
in the playground, where mothers
watch their children swing
on monkey bars above the sand.

When she was lifted onto the gurney,
the rising sun highlighted
gray hair among the brown,
like mine, falling to her shoulders.

Did the policemen blame me
for the body almost on my doorstep?
I heard nothing in the night.
Standing there, I couldn't look into her face.

Wakeful on Thirty-third Street

Walking in the rain before dawn,
I smell petals opening, slip
on their fallen bodies, and watch
the fast-moving storm clear
to reveal a half-moon, a few stars.
Rivers surge under the streets.

The only man to stop and talk
has a radar mount on the front
of an old Cadillac and a desert
mine full of raw diamonds to
protect him when the promised
invasion from the sky begins.

We each watch the sky.
Tensed for change, I've begun
to expect meteor showers
and comets and blazing
sunrises, anything to sweep me
along fevered morning walks.

Neither of us can sleep,
me—because I'm forty and believe
time moves around me at light speed,
pulling me out of bed with the song
of an unpartnered nightingale
filling the wet, dark air.

The stranger wants to give me a small diamond,
and I want to accept his protection against the unknown.

What Does the New Moon Hide From?

Dogs barking at a skateboard rasping
across the dark. The mother scolding
her children to bed. A house where the wife
is beaten. Tonight it is silent. May God
keep her safe. The daughter leaving home,
the door closed on her soft goodnight
spoken in the dark. Golden gingko leaves
on wet pavement caught by headlights.
Motion detectors blinking on
over garage doors. Wet tires
slipping on streets. Trains whistling directions
along distant rails. Airplanes seeking
their places in landing patterns.
Wood smoke hovering around chimneys.
Sweet iris blooming in a false November
spring. The silence after a rainstorm.

In the Light

For Joe Millar

He sits on a concrete stoop
to smoke a cigarette,
his hair silvered by the street lamp,
his back slumped,
a soft, leather-covered book
on the cold step beside him.

He unzips the black book that
reminds me of a Bible
my sister had when she was little.
The zipper protected
the red dye of Christ's words
when she left it in the rain.

Perhaps he's looking for a passage
to open Sunday's sermon;
this man could be as at home
in a sweeping robe
as in blue jeans. Or he might
be looking for comfort.

When he unzips the book and takes
a pen out, he fills
lined paper with tiny script,
poetry as wide as the page.
He holds the only words that count
in his hands.

One More Draft

Poetry finds the entry to the crawlspace beneath
the house, carrying shiny copper pipes
to replace rusted galvanized conduits
that brought water in.
Though on his knees, he balances

the pipes and his tools and enters the dark.
I can hear him there, under the floorboards,
under the joists, moving past the concrete piers
the whole house rests on.
He understands valves and u-joints and diverters,

recognizes where relieving pressure
on one line will plug up another.
He has been known to put his back out under there,
lying with his spine on the wet clay or resting
his belly in tight places while he stretches

his arms to reach the next joint with a wrench.
When he packs up his tools and the old pipes,
leaving the air filled with sweated copper
and a day's toil, I open the faucets. The water
flows, fast and clear.

Slow Burn

Downsizing

The streets are littered
with middle management, cut loose
from walnut desks by another
reduction in force, almost
as many as out-of-work poets.
It's a muse's market out here,
and I can have any poet I choose,
maybe even settle down
with one writer for a while,
somebody offering fringe benefits,
say, gourmet coffee and an appreciation
of fine old forms, like sestinas—

a poet hungry for company
and comfortable with words,
blooming calla lilies, and sudden death—

a poet curious about line breaks,
sprays of lilac in a green glass vase,
and the scent of evil on a back road—

a poet persistent in seeking the perfect
rhythm, an unblemished peach,
and the warmth of carefully banked coals.

This time, I get to choose,
and I'm tired of passionate hotheads.
I'm looking for a poet capable
of a long, slow burn.

Down the Mountain

Escaping from a weekend
with five hundred singles,
Sunday morning, I start down
from Hume Lake, where clouds
touch the ground.
I lose the redwoods at 3,000 feet
and enter scrub-oak territory
on my way to the Central Valley.
I cannot lose them fast enough.

Under cloudless, growing-season skies,
the radio can be tuned into sermons
or Mexican polkas.
I lean a small notebook
against the steering wheel
and dig for a pencil in my purse
to take notes about my flight
from prayers for marriage
and lectures on dating etiquette.

The wind throws bugs
against the windshield
and pushes the car
toward the slow lane.
Traffic skims over
the two-lane blacktop
with its faded white arrows,
which seem to say,
no one escapes, but here, try.

The truckers and I pass over
tomatoes from overloaded trucks
that can afford to spill
parts of their cash crops,
and we catch moths bright
as pats of butter in our grills.
We hurry to leave behind air laden
with manure and grapes ripening
to sugar on the vines.

Fast-food billboards block
my view of the orange groves.
Finally, I give in
and relieve the heat
with a Dairy Queen Blizzard,
Butterfinger candy whirled
into vanilla ice cream.

And slip back to summer nights
in Tennessee when Daddy
stopped for Dairy Queen
on the way home
from my grandparents' house,
so large it was once a hotel—
all white wood and deep porches,
where there was always too much
family and too little privacy.

Now one billboard asks me
to *Choose Chowchilla*
but never says what for,
Chowchilla—a town no larger than

Tennessee City, where my grandparents
died. So I blow by the town
where Costco's parking lot
is fuller than that
of the Living Fountain Church.

Cirrus clouds build
and, briefly, rain
spatters the windshield—
breaking humidity,
pushing down
the scent of the hay harvest,
washing away
the bodies of smashed,
winged insects.

My next break is Turlock rest stop,
where vending machines dispense
caffeine and Excedrin,
disposable diapers and Modesto maps.
Only children notice
the adjacent grove of almond trees
and try to climb the fence.
Newspaper stands, emptied
of *S. F. Chronicles*, hold *Modesto Bees*.

I have only to cross
the Altamont Pass to be all
the way down, where clouds
cast shadows on golden grass,
while windmills on the ridge
seem to drag the clouds down
to the ground, where they go dark.
City lights will beckon me,
guide me home.

Beauty Ranch

Panting, I breach the trees
for the meadow. Feet leave
behind the dirt, moist and fecund,
packed beneath needles and oak leaves
in the shadow of redwoods
clustered around the burnt-out
trunk of a sister. Feet step
softly where owl's clover springs
along the side of a muddy path.

Horses marked the trail
with dung; their hooves
stirred up mud where damselflies
flit low, green and blue,
ahead of footsteps.
The first dragonfly
of the season flies out of reach.
No one leans against me out of breath
at the end of my quick climb.

Around the pond, it's not the fur
of a fallen animal caught
in a fallen tree limb
but the fuzz of cattails
blown from stalks by spring wind
and rain. New reeds along the bank
add to the green decay
that floats on the water.

It is never silent here—
the wind carries—
wolf howls of boys
who quickly move on,
birds calling
attention away from nests
in the middle of the pond,
fish leaping
for dinner while they ignore
hooks before them,

lizards running
from exposure in the sun
to shelter in fallen trees,
and endless grasses making
their way through soft green muck.
A stream carries running
water beneath the flat, shifting
surface.

Branches creak. Leaves rustle.
I know how to be alone here.
A red hawk catches an updraft,
where sunshine and shadow are both God.
I push the bay-tree branch
away from my face.

Alluvial Changes

The delta stills in this shallow curve,
silt-brown water under a blue sky,
no reflection of the sky like the ocean,
no reflection of the pines like a lake,
the underwater slope so gentle
that the wakes of boats only softly
make the river's mouth rock and shimmer,
with its black and gold lights,
reflecting only color, no images.

Here the river, old, slow-moving,
shifts—not yet ready for the sea change.
Not yet ready to leave the delta behind
for the depths of saltwater.

The murky water must be walked into
to be known, toes exploring silken mud,
rocks few and far between and smooth.
I stand ankle-deep in the water
and cannot see my toes,
then sit in the warmth up to my neck,
giving only as much of myself
to the water or the sun as I choose.
And then, the sudden drop.

Holy Places

—Saint Francis in Ecstasy, *Bellini*

I.

The cave of blue stones eddies with joy,
as barefoot before God, Saint Francis
opens his arms to greet the invisible Creator,
whom he has come so far to hear,
leaving behind the crenellated towers
of the hilltop castle and its fortified town,
to shelter here in a cave with a skull and a Bible,
the Word made flesh and the flesh perished.
A rabbit, donkey, and egret witness
the divine visitation, while in a distant field,
a shepherd continues to herd his flock
toward town as twilight nears.

II.

At San Diego de Alcalá, in a cell
as white as the cave is blue, Friar Junipero Serra
left his ecstasy behind him too.
In his cool retreat, he stored the treasures
of monastic life—a table, a chair,
a bed with no mattress, and a perpetual Sunday peace
woven of his whispered reading
of scripture as he sounded the words,
the chant of his rosary and clack of beads,
moans of a penitent who would have crawled
the length of the New World
to bring people to God.

III.

Is it possible my ecstasy still moves unrecognized
along Kitchen Creek, flying green among dragonflies —
above mesquite, small lizards, and the narrow stream
between hot, flat stones? If God spoke there,
he did not call me beyond the moment, to lead
animals or heathens to him,
and it was neither white-hot nor distant blue.
I heard only the indecipherable stream and the
chittering squirrels among the unguarded miners' stakes.
Ecstasy became the fear of a brushfire, the glory
of the sun's light passing through the dragonfly's wings,
touching its fragmented eyes.

Austere Essentials of the Palette

At dawn, the comet stops riding
over Kitchen Mesa. In the cobalt
blue sky, stars disappear,
as the crust of frost beneath
my feet does, under the sun.

That blue of God's eye forces
my eyes down and fills them
with desert color: iron red,
oxide yellow, pyromorphite green,
broad strokes of pigment in sandstone.

O'Keeffe spent a lifetime not quite
getting these colors right, so turned
instead to cattle bones and flowers
that could only have broken into
blossom in less-harsh sunlight.

Chimney Rock, carved by wind and rain,
stands erect above the tops
of mesas that thrust their way
out of the high plains, reaching
for water and God.

When I start my hike,
Chimney Rock seems days, not hours, away.
Sharp in my lungs as I climb,
air convinces me that no one inhales
this land and exhales it onto paper.

In this territory, where snow
melts slowly in crevices sun never
reaches, O'Keeffe kept surfaces flat—
from red dirt roads to spirals of rock.
No one is ever large enough,

only rock is substantive. In canyons,
a whisper echoes off stone to become
a whirling winter storm of words.
The only painting where O'Keeffe came close,
done long before she knew the desert,

is a blue line splitting a white-paper field
and pooling at the bottom.

Some Stars Are Not Used for Navigation

On the bay, the waters stir as the sun goes down
and stones along the shore are beaten by the tide,
as the pine windbreak is beaten by the rising winds,
and the sailors who fished at the world's edge
all day surrender their boats to the dusk waves
as gulls surrender their wings to the dusk sky.

He waits for still waters and a star-marked sky,
lingers over beer and sandwiches, the sails down.
The fear of his own freedom out here hits him in waves.
There are enough hard-boiled detective books below to tide
him over until the endless mirror of the open ocean can edge
him into dreams, where portholes are windows

and hatches are doors and the endless sea
winds, like a lawn, around the boat, out to meet the sky,
and offers him a cool place to lie on the edge
of death until he tires of swimming and slips down
to become bloated flotsam on a rising tide,
to discover a lighter gravity riding the waves.

A last fishing trawler motors by; sailors wave
at him, their yellow slickers pulled tight against wind
and spray, as their prow bounces on the tide.
They are mostly shadow and light against a sky
no longer pink with the glow of a smog-filtered sundown.
With the trawler, night has come over the world's edge.

He finishes his after-dinner pipe, moves back from the edge,
packs away fear and freedom, as waves
become quiet and the wind settles down.
He decides it is time to head home and rewinds
the ropes that hold him still beneath the sky.
He wants no more lonely rising and ebbing of tides

that leave his mind a vortex of flood tides.
From now on, he'll race, on the edge
of competition, sails tight against a sunny sky,
a crew to stand with him before the waves,
a crew to stand and shelter him from the winds,
to help him haul the canvas up and down.

He rides high on the tide. His motor skims the waves,
as ahead and to his right, the edge of the shoreline unwinds
before his eyes, and stars in the sky begin to rain down.

The Catch

Simon Peter sits in the silver
of his fish nets, uses bare toes
to pull the next tear closer
as he bends his silver hair closer
in fading light to the net
and the needle.
He mends the net
because he must—

without remembering how the net,
leaving the boat, spreads
and drops into the lake,
bright on the lake before dawn,
without remembering the weight
of the full net, pulled back
into the boat brimming
with fish for market.

Christ has yet to ask him
to become a fisher of men,

to bring his brother with him
to spend years walking dusty roads.

Peter has yet to deny
his God three times before

the crow of dawn, with a fear
he does not even know now.

Shattered

You know how hard it is sometimes just to walk on the streets
downtown, how everything enters you
the way scientists describe it—photons streaming through . . .

—"Quantum," Kim Addonizio

Never sit in a Broadway cafe with your back
to the door. For though the man who comes through
it raves about wanting his gun, he cannot harm you
if his eyes enter your world, where dinner brings
only the calm lifting of chicken soup to your mouth,
the careful sopping of broth with a buttered roll.
What enters you is the starless aspect
of his skyscraper alleys, the chill of wind forced
through concrete corridors, the refrain, "I need my gun.
They'd understand that. All of them. They'd understand that."
What enters you is cold neon lighting reflected
in the window. What enters you is the hollow rumble
of a truck on an empty street that starts the cafe window
next to him vibrating, sets up a harmonic resonance
that shatters that window and silences him—as diamond-
perfect shards fall around his feet. What enters you
are tiny pieces of glass—prisms for light,
razor-edged, made from sand and returning to sand
there on the black-and-white floor.

Federal Building Bombed

We lifted pieces of skyscraper
in Oklahoma City, pushed
aside mangled tricycles to hand
children, who couldn't remember their names,
to ambulance workers. Sirens never
stopped. But nothing got through to
my numbed body, sorting
glass from flesh and cement,
until a volunteer put a cup of coffee
in my hands.
No lid to hold
in the heat,
and I wept,
faced with
the only grief
I could put my
hands around.

Nicodemus

The wind blows wherever it pleases. You can hear its sound,
but you cannot tell where it comes from or where it is going.
So it is with everyone born of the spirit.

—John 3:8 NIV

We wrapped his body in aloe
to heal our burns,
pressed myrrh between his burial cloths,
where it will deaden our pain.

And still I cannot answer his riddle:

No one can enter the Kingdom of God
unless he is born again of the water and the spirit.

Trapped in a place as dark as the womb,
I can hear but cannot feel the wind against me.

Acknowledgments

"Pacific Bell Comes Calling," *Apple Valley Review*
"What Does the New Moon Hide From?" *Ragazine*
"Celibacy," *Glint Literary Journal*
"Once Begun," *California Quarterly*
"Last Prayer," *The Stand*
"Open Reading, Shattuck Avenue Bakery," *East Bay Review*
"Some Stars Are Not Used for Navigation," *Obsession: Sestinas in the Twenty-First Century*
"The Road Alone," *BorderSenses*
"Federal Building Bombed," *Whirlwind Magazine*
"Winter Departure," *The Phoenix Rising from the Ashes*
"Down the Road," *Verse Wisconsin*
"Sand and Ash," *Palimpsest Journal*
"Lecture Devant la Fenetre Ouverte," *The Stillwater Review*
"Peaceable Kingdom," *The Chaffin Journal*
"Wife of a Prison Gardener," *Off the Coast*
"Angel Island, San Francisco," *The Same*
"One More Draft," *Red Rock Review*
"Una Jeffers' Tower" as "Tower" and "Tor House," *Black Fox Review*

"Austere Essentials," *Studio*

"Monarchs" as "Low Tide," *Steam Ticket*

"Invocation" as "Dusk," *Generations*

"Sweet Contamination," *Evening Street Review*

"Infectious Paranoia," *Not One of Us*

"Difficult to Place," *The Village Pariah*

"Threat of Drowning," *Knocking at the Door: Poems about Approaching the Other*

"Eclipse," *Midwest Literary Magazine*

"No Clemency," *Milk Money*

"After the Fireworks" as "Just Sparklers," *Ouroboros Review*

"Prayers for the Barren," *Thirty-first Bird Review*

"Distracted," *Reed Magazine*

"In the Light," *Main Street Rag*

"The Catch," *Stray Light*

Published long ago and far away under the maiden name Trina Baker:

"Hunger Moon," *Westview*

"Beauty Ranch" as "Redemption," *Perspectives: A Journal of Reformed Thought*

"Spring Incantation" and "Winter Departure," *Yemassee*

"Shattered," *Natural Bridge*

"Through Her Husband's Eyes," *The Sierra Nevada College Review*

"Downsizing," *MO: Writings from the River*

"Submerged," *Slant*

"Language Lessons," *Coracle*

"Spring in the City," *City Works '01*

"Alluvial Changes," in *Poetic Medicine*, by John Fox

Title Index

A

After the Fireworks 53
Alluvial Changes 78
Angel Island, San Francisco 45
Austere Essentials of the Palette 81

B

Badlands 52
Beauty Ranch 76

C

Celibacy 50

D

Difficult to Place 58
Distracted 34
Downsizing 72
Down the Mountain 73
Down the Road 56

E

Eclipse 64

Eventide, Naomi 23

F

Federal Building Bombed 87

H

Holy Places 79

Hunger Moon 65

I

Infectious Paranoia 42

In the Light 68

Invocation 11

L

Language Lessons 55

Last Prayer 37

Lecture Devant la Fenetre Ouverte 60

M

Migration Routes 15

Monarchs 33

N

Nicodemus 88

No Clemency 19

O

October 59

Offering Respite 38

Once Begun 54

One More Draft 69

Open Reading, Shattuck Avenue Bakery 44

P

Pacific Bell Comes Calling 43

Peaceable Kingdom 20

Prayers for the Barren 61

R

Rear Window 41

S

Sand and Ash 32

Shattered 86

Snow Melts, Tennessee 17

Some Stars Are Not Used for Navigation 83

Spring Incantation 14

Spring in the City 40

Submerged 30

Sweet Contamination 21

T

The Catch 85

The Road Alone 49

The Threat of Drowning 25

Through Her Husband's Eyes 24

Tor House 47

U

Una Jeffers' Tower 48

W

Wakeful on Thirty-third Street 66

What Does the New Moon Hide From? 67

Wife of a Prison Gardener 28

Winter Departure 36

First Line Index

A

After camping alone for a week 53

A moment ago, Lee sat at the table 47

Asked about the day of my birth 19

At dawn, the comet stops riding 81

Awake with a new design, I walk 32

B

Before she clasps 21

C

Chasing the last of summer 33

D

David's never seen a goat pen before 20

Dogs barking at a skateboard rasping 67

Down south, Mama keeps a trio 15

E

Eating oranges, she crossed Death Valley 52

Escaping from a weekend 73

G

God, I can gather Lincoln roses in my arms and 37

H

He comes in, hidden in the 59

He drives up in a Pac Bell truck 43

He lights a cigarette 58

He sits on a concrete stoop 68

I

It stains my forefinger and fills my nails 54

L

Learn the names of all you love—quince, rose, grace 14

N

Never sit in a Broadway cafe with your back 86

No rarity, lunar eclipses 64

November 61

O

Once again, rain falls late into the night 40

On the bay, the waters stir as the sun goes down 83

P

Panting, I breach the trees 76

Poetry finds the entry to the crawlspace beneath 69

R

Remember her 24

Robert climbs the secret stairs of the tower last 48

S

She doesn't walk down to the beach 28

She thought they were making love 50

Simon Peter sits in the silver 85

Soft family whispers 11

T

That full moon catches 41

The cave of blue stones eddies with joy 79

The dalmatian eats with horses 17

The delta stills in this shallow curve 78

The early light reflects the short gray hairs 36

The first morning spring winds 38

The island watches the moss grow 45

The new manager is atwitter 44

The sea spits him back out at the end 25

The streets are littered 72

The sun shines away the window frame 60

The third time, to reach her it hid 30

The tiny mother leaves a daycare job 56

The upper room of the church holds 55

This morning, that full hunger 65

This year, when the lily of the Nile blooms 42

Tonight, with my eyes tired 23

Traveling the Camino Real 49

W

Walking in the rain before dawn 66

We lifted pieces of skyscraper 87

We wrapped his body in aloe 88

Y

You pull ripe tomatoes 34

Printed in the USA
CPSIA information can be obtained
at www.ICGtesting.com
LVHW030715100724
785064LV00003B/8

9 781594 981340